FOREST BO

STEP HUMAN INTO THIS WORLD

OLAV MÜNZBERG, born in 1938 in Gleiwitz (Gliwice), fled with his family to southern Germany as a result of the turbulence of World War II. He has lived in Berlin since 1962. He studied Law and obtained his PhD in Comparative Religion, Aesthetics and German Literature at the Free University of Berlin. He works as a writer, art critic for the *Berliner Kunstblatt* and organizer of art exhibits. Since 1974 he has been co-editor of the magazine *Ästhetik und Kommunikation* (with L. Wilkens since 1981, Frankfurt). At present he is chairman of the Union of Writers in Berlin. Since 1973 he has worked on several publications, including 'The Difficulty of Making Art' (co-edited with H. Pfütze, 1973, Suhrkamp, Frankfurt), 'Entrances and Exits' (poems, 1975, Berlin), 'I close the door and begin to live' (poems and short prose, 1983, Berlin), 'Diego Rivera 1886–1957' (co-edited with M. Nungesser, 1987, Berlin), 'From the Old West to the Culture Forum: The Tiergarten Quarter in Berlin' (editor, 1988, Berlin), 'Malet: Literature from Malta' (co-editor and translator, 1989, Berlin).

MITCH COHEN, born in 1952 in Pasadena, California, studied English Language & Literature at the University of California and German Literature at the Free University Berlin. He has lived in Germany since 1975, and in Berlin since 1977. After several years instructing children in art and ceramics, he now works as a freelance translator and writer. His publications include: 'ondas: an anthology of Santa Barbara Poets' (editor, 1974, Santa Barbara), 'Ber!in: contemporary writing from East and West Berlin' (editor and translator, 1983, Banda Books, Santa Barbara), as well as numerous contributions to anthologies, magazines and radio in Germany, America, Austria and France.

HANS CHRISTOPH BUCH, born in Wetzlar, has been working in Berlin as a freelance writer since 1964. As well as numerous stories and essays, he has published a novel, 'The Wedding at Port-au-Prince' (1984) which has been translated into several languages (English 1987).

Olav Münzberg

Step Human into this World

Für den unermüdlichen
„Fotografen"
Sir Peter Fisher
from the Insel Wight
Gedichte im weltbürger-

TRAVEL POEMS BY

Olav Münzberg

Translated from the German by Mitch Cohen
new poems translated by Ingrid Stoll

licher „das heißt humani-
tärer Absicht" (J. Kant)

Melnik (Bulgarien)
Festival der Literatur
Berlin
10. – 11.10.
2003

Olav Münzberg

FOREST
BOOKS
London & Boston

PUBLISHED BY
FOREST BOOKS
20 Forest View, Chingford, London E4 7AY, U.K.
61 Lincoln Road, Wayland, MA 01778, U.S.A.

FIRST PUBLISHED 1991

Typeset in Great Britain by Cover to Cover, Cambridge
Printed in Great Britain by BPCC Wheatons Ltd, Exeter

ISBN No. 0 948259 53 1

British Library Cataloguing in Publication Data
Münzberg, Olav, 1938——
Step human into this world: travel poems
I. Title   II. Cohen, Mitchell, 1952   III. Stoll, Ingrid
New poems
831.914

Library of Congress Catalogue Card No.
90–81862

Contents

Foreword

Olav Münzberg is a native Silesian who migrated via Franconia to Berlin, a qualified lawyer who studied philosophy, a philosopher who writes poetry. A two- nay three-fold 'alienation'. In addition to his Law and Philosophy studies, which he completed with a doctorate on the aesthetic subject in Kant, Hegel and Adorno, he has played in a jazz orchestra and a street theatre group, organised art exhibitions, written essays and articles, and travelled extensively, from Greece to Egypt, from the USA to Mexico. He has worked for the *Neue Gesellschaft für Literatur* (the 'New Society for Literature') for many years, and been President of the *Berliner Schriftstellerverband* ('Berlin Writers' Association') since 1989.

I first met Olav Münzberg twenty-five years ago in a West Berlin jazz club. He was studying Law, and in his free time he played the clarinet and devoted himself to literature and philosophy. In 1969, at the height of the students' revolt, we met again as members of a street theatre group which was proclaiming the socialist cause: not the 'real existing' socialism of Moscow or East Germany, but the socialist utopia of Marx and Engels which had passed through the critical filter of the Frankfurt School. Olav was playing the part of the Capitalist who, with his top hat and cigar, paunch and watch chain, symbolized the 'restoration of capital' in the Federal Republic of Germany. In another play, which we performed in front of factory gates during the wildcat strikes, he represented the agitator who, in the tones of the preacher rather than a propagandist, shook people out of their lethargy and challenged them to take self-determined action: it wasn't until later that student protests degenerated into terrorism.

Olav Münzberg has remained faithful to the utopias of 1968: undogmatic, open and radical, but also — and this too is a legacy of the students' movement — critical to the point of self-criticism and theory-conscious to the point of top-heaviness. Kant and Hegel, Marx and Freud, Marcuse and

Adorno, Brecht and Benjamin — these were the intellectual 'superfathers' of our generation to whom Olav Münzberg paid tribute in his thesis; later came the artists of the Mexican Revolution, José Clemente Orozco and Diego Rivera, and the ideas of the women's and ecology movements. Olav Münzberg's poems express great feeling towards the survivors of the Holocaust and other victims of German history (his commentary on the poems of his mother, Elisabeth Münzberg, is one of the most moving texts he has written). They also express the internationalism of 1968 and solidarity with the poor and the oppressed of the Third world. Yet the hidden *leitmotiv* in his poetry is an aesthetic fascination with the works of nature and art, from ancient to modern, in which hope transcends the terrors of the past — hope which, in the words of Ernst Bloch, is indestructible: 'Home is, where nobody yet was'. It is in this spirit that Olav Münzberg's poetry should be read.

Hans Christoph Buch
Berlin, December 1990

Translator's Note

Whether taken as a noun or as an adjective – in his title, Olaz Münzberg leaves the word *Mensch* (human) playfully ambiguous – whether as a form of address or as a description as to how one is to 'step into this world', these poems ask again and again the question 'What is human, what is the human being?' With friendly envy, the poet contrasts the effortless flight of the ponto birds in Mexico with the difficult and technologically mediated flight of humans – who, however, fly higher and further. If being human is, first of all, not having the advantages of other creatures but rather our own, these poems are still neither a paeon to an automatic Progress nor to Man as Lord of Creation. Münzberg and his poems are far too interested in history and the realities surrounding us for either of these complacent faiths. Look, the poems say, at who and where we are. Friendliness to humanity is their salient characteristic, but they are not congratulatory.

If the poet's allegiance is to Humanism and to the tradition of the Enlightenment, then not in the abstract, not as a matter of good tone or purely ideological conviction – that is to say, not as a stance – but in the daily interaction between the world and his senses, including the vital organs heart and brain: that is, as a gait.

In my country, poets are exhorted to capture the 'spirit of place' and have Williams' dictum in their ear: 'No ideas but in things'. Williams' warning that he didn't mean the poet must 'shut up his mind in a corncrib' is often forgotten. Many of Münzberg's poems are meditations on inconspicuous details, things specific to their locations, but the ideas are never sleeping and Münzberg attends to place in many places. Münzberg's own city, Berlin, and its history from the end of the War to the end of the Wall are viewed with the same curious, questioning eye as are Egypt or Mexico and their histories. Home only reveals its quiet secrets, whether tragic, nasty, ironic or beautiful, to eyes that don't assume they know their home; and the big world beyond your own little world is still your world, if you don't assume it cannot speak with you.

Mitch Cohen

Note:

Most of the Berlin poems were written in the seventies and eighties, with several added in November 1989. The poems about Mexico are taken from 'I close the door and begin to live' published in Berlin in 1983; the poems about books are a reaction to the existential crisis of the book brought about by the new mass media. The poems under the title 'The human stepping into the world' were written in the last two years. The poems about Egypt were produced during my journey there in 1986. The poems about Malta I wrote on my trip to that island in 1987.

Olav Münzberg
1990

1
Berlin

Prussian general

Ordering
and
obeying
were written
into him
in his body
From his situation
he sprang
away
from Democracy
into his dream —
Dictatorship
Even
with his arm torn off
his sights
are set on
this insanity

(M.C.)

Bit of a wall

1945 material
exploded into the wall
Death beside it
Now
a wounded tree stands up
and goes
across the border

(M.C.)

Harmless grass

The glance
has
gone to the ground
A head
lies
on the pavement
and bleeds outwards
The proximity is striking
Only a few paving stones
are camouflaged
white

(M.C.)

Berlin Tiergarten Sigismundstrasse House Nr. 4a[1]

The only
house surviving
What stood next to it
was destroyed
by the war
The only
house surviving
as if it were
without an inside
mere façade
Scent of decomposition

The only
house still surviving
What stood next to it
was torn down
as if it were
dispersing
swaying stone
splintered glass
for the interested glance
inhabitant-free
Whoever
was there
was
dispersed into another housing bunker

The only
house still living
and the space next to it
have been gripped by
reeling clouds
In the late afternoon
for the wink of an eye
comes
magic for a visit

4

if the sky goes
through the panes
it looks
as if
twilight and verdigris
had arrived
on the façade

(M.C.)

Without homeland

Drift-ice in Berlin
The moraines
return
after many years
again
Green dies out

(M.C.)

Remembrance of Aunt Lotte
or
The Class Question

This
is not the way someone stands
who owns a house
behind the door
This
is not the way someone glances
who owns a house
behind the door
This
is not the way someone glances
who owns a house
through the smashed glass rib
of a Berlin wooden door
This
only silent any more
is how someone protests
before her death
against
a prescribed life
killed
with rented space

(M.C.)

Farewell to the tiled stove

Retreat
is blocked
downfall in its place

has warmth
stepped into the wall
Farewell

Farewell
to cuddling
my back
on the stone mother
against the pressing cold
Farewell once more
later
the uncomfortable ribs
of the new heater
sometime

(M.C.)

What was Berlin in 1960?

The necessity of a license to move here
for inhabitants of West Germany
What was Kreuzberg?
The shop window of a
second-hand store
A pair of dice
cost 5 pfennigs
a tie
worn for at least ten years
twenty-five pfennigs
but one
of which one couldn't say
whether one wanted to have it
and a comb
thirty pfennigs
Nothing more lay in
the shop window

(M.C.)

Berlin in a whirl[2]

Berlin is in a whirl,
I mean both halves of the city.
The 750-year jubilee has turned them on
like a calcified water faucet
that, despite all efforts,
cannot be turned off.
It's bubbling here:
who is the greatest?
Who polishes up the city the cleanest?
Who covers up scandals the best?
Who deals best with glitter?
Who can draw the most tourists into the city?
Who does the most business?
Can event Y be outdone by X?
Berlin is a screamer. That goes for West as well as for East.
That the presidents arrive is part of the etiquette.
That each is right is provided for in the protocol
and in the entry in the respective golden or red book
                                        of the city.
Berlin celebrates up toward the Wall
from both sides.
That there were and are victims
is swallowed down with the respective breakfast coffees
and, at noon at the latest,
eliminated into the canals.
Berlin celebrates
and plays down
that it once was the centre of terror
for Germany, Europe, and the world.
This theme is approached only with repressed distaste.
If it were possible
it would like most of all
to forget that torment.

                                        (M.C.)

Never again Berlin

Someone got off there
a tourist
some crows from Russia
at the former Potsdamer Platz[3]
Someone is bitching there
Someone throws away his lover
or just his declaration of love
Someone abdicates there
like Wilhelm the Second on November 9, 1918

Never again will the Kaiser ride
through the Tiergarten in a coach
or celebrate his bull sessions in the Hotel Esplanade
with the military and nobility
never again monarchy
never again Weimar Republic[4]
never again 'Third Reich'[5]

If the Second World War weren't
ended in Germany on May 8, 1945,
in which the Soviets played a decisive role,
probably three months later
the first atomic bomb would have fallen on Berlin.
Never again Hiroshima, would then
have been Never again Berlin

Sitting on this city, of course, are rage and anger and hate
toward this megalomania 'Germania'[6]
toward Himmler Goebbels and Eichmann
never again Berlin
never again Wannsee Conference and 'Final Solution'[7]
never again the Reich Security Headquarters and
Prinz Albrechstrasse[8]
this torture 'palace'
What an absurdity
and again and again in every individual fate

Golgotha
Never again Coventry
Never again Hitler and Nazi Germany

Never again Berlin swore former
Jewish 'co-citizens'
escapees from the humiliation
the abasement the annihilation
Fifty years later, some have
ventured into Berlin again
the city of mourning
the city of liberation
the organizing centre of the abyss
not just nights of bombs
not just the howling of sirens
not just the deportations
at S-Bahn[9] station Grunewald and at the
Beuseelbrücke in Moabit

Never again Berlin
so they sat in the train or in the cattle car
and thought, in the beginning, of resettlement
of a kind of banishment or of a different
work place
Never again
swore thousands
if not millions
and what remains of that?

What was worked through
what was merely quickly buried and
levelled in the Tiergarten quarter and at
Potsdamer Platz
in Stadt-Mitte and in Prenzlauer Berg[10]
What was torn down
in the Soviet occupied sector and in the
British French and American occupied
sectors as

self-punishment or as if it
were a penance
in mutual rage
as rage against the architecture of the 19th century
as if that had set the stage for National Socialism
with pomp and ostentation

And what was rehabilitated along with the goose-step
and what in the childish game of postmodern quotationitis
appearing harmless
only a window sill falls away from Stirling[11]
With the Speer quotation and
mountings are cyclopianly dismantled

What is really so fascinating in
acts of emptying
in abstractions into emptiness
in downfalls of the self
in the so-called 'Being of What Is'[12]
in self-important reverence
in the mannerism of magic
in brutal animal power
in empty greatnesses and in
militarily vertical monumentalized
construction masses

Are the fascinations of
acts of emptying
merely the other side of
losses of closeness
of uncompleted separations
from the mother
Illusionary reversals of the caves of origin
that never return
and then end up in cults of
death and ruins and destruction and self-destruction

Eichmann's mountains of files
have vanished
but what goes on in the computers of individual
states of this earth?
Berlin has become uninteresting
compared with the problems of the ending 20th
and approaching 21st centuries
Berlin is a spot on this earth
like others like Tashkent or Toronto
and yet it carries the pain of separation as a
relict

Berlin has become more modest
and must remain so
only then will it overcome its inner separation
only then will it become a living
democratic city
cooperating in the continuance of
the human species and its unity

Never again Berlin or
just Berlin
The Japanese embassy in the old
Tiergartenstrasse, today's whores' street,
was reconstructed as it was originally
The yellow clayish slabs were delivered
from the same quarry by the
same company
Never again Berlin?

On the Hall of Soldiers planned by Speer
stands the Philharmonie by Hans Scharoun
Music in the place of the childishness of 'playing guns'
and a cult of weapons
extended into adulthood
On the old Reich Highway Nr 1
Aachen–Königsberg
stands the State Library by the same architect

The floor plan consists of a pistol
but it's filled with books
not with powder

Crows in the old Potsdamer Strasse
that has become a dead end
Arbors and training lots for German shepherds
At the 'Weinhaus Huth', the last house on
Potsdamer Platz, it's said
a new restaurant will open

New life in Berlin
Berlin on its way
life again in the old place?

(M.C.)

Corner

Without noticing it
the lion has
eaten
little green
inconspicuous moulds
In the ruins of Prussia
his game
against the birds
is lost

(M.C.)

Berlin Wall

What's breaking through now?
Kant?
'Das Kapital'?
The early Marx?
The middle Freud?
The figure three?
I do not know.
The suture
which ran across the town
has come apart.

(I.S.)

History's I.O.U.

Lost
in a self-mutilated city
The Trabants[13] have arrived.

The bottom-line on
history's I.O.U. is still
not drawn.

Everywhere bodies
in high waters.
The ice-block
has given way to drift-ice
not only
in the glitzy part of town

Twenty-eight years of
blocked railway crossing.
Did we stand all the time
before its closed barriers?
Did a train pass at all?
Who were the passengers
and what was the load?

(I.S.)

I see for myself therefore I am

Congestion
built-up since 1933 and
continuously
rising since 1945
a flood of declarations now
down the heaped-up history
tenacious like discharge of lava
Feet furiously crossed the border
hands pulled the exhausted body
up the walls of embassies
others climbed over fences
swam across rivers and
spent the nights in the usual fear
a Chinese June dragon
at their backs which
rose with the wind of autumnal pictures
chilling and
paralysing.

The double images
of a constant schizophrenia
have been followed
by renunciation
of its enforcement
the mock spring cleaning
followed the opening of windows in autumn
Fear shaken off
like the removal of a foreign hand
which lay heavily on shoulders.
The 'Critical Theory'[14] —
declared out-stripped in the West
although not out-dated —
is now moving into the East
tentatively.

Now, it's:
I go by myself
therefore I am.

I speak for myself
therefore I think.

I vote
therefore I decide.

At places of mourning
the light of candles
the light of dialogue
the light of demonstrations
and in remembrance of
the beginning of the 2nd World War
50 years ago on 1.9.1989
the conscience of millions of Germans
is stirred again.

The congestion is dissolving
in houses of the Nikolai district
in streets around Alexander Square
and the neck is freed of the wrong scarf
the throat cleared of tirades of
ideologies
after constant fighting
a bloc goes free
and with it a country.

(I.S.)

Night from 9th to 10th November 1989
— Jogging in Berlin —

The stone on the wall
splits

White trainers
by which you will recognize citizens of the GDR
and pale jeans

6.57 pm
8.10 pm
10.31 pm

These moments
in which millions
hear about happenings
yesterday hardly thought possible
and which they — with beaming eyes —
tell neighbours
complete strangers
and children.

Many, now reeling
torn out of sleep
by frenzied ringing
and excited telephone calls

This dropping of everything
and this breathlessness and
lowering of car windows

Now, here and then
after 28 years
Now, with dreams
in one's arms
Now, away from those leaps
into death
away from those shots

that killed
and away from the picture of a sworn enemy
that prevented living side by side.

Those cold feet
overrunning borders
are warming up
Those many voices
which turn hoarse
in this cloudless night
Catching cold
nobody minds
The sleepless freedom
suddenly in the midst of the town
soundless and exuberant
and again and again
standing still in amazement
in tumultuous streets
in telephone cables, telex machines
and pictures
which are sent into all corners of the world.

This shock wave in the limbs and
in the head, waves of emotions in the whole
body
This numbing of the taboo
This putting to rest
of an unbending power
These exits of masters of mummies
this end of outdated and
ill-conceived prophecies
that this monstrous wall will still be
there for the next hundred years

This sense of wonder
that there is a different life.

The throat is now being stuffed anew
for a start with simple things
the first pizza
the first doner kebab
the first Greek sheep cheese
and the first West Berliner curried hot-dog
from Italy and from Turkey
from Greece and from the other part of
Germany.

(I.S.)

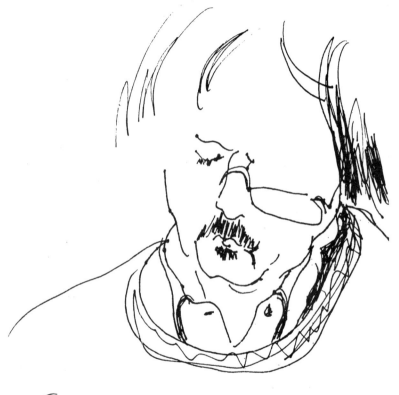

JS|89

2
Mexico

Isla Mujeres I

The beach
of warm snow.
Snow above
and below water.
Snow in the sky.
Snow,
the gossamer of trees.
Snow,
and again Caribbean snow
in this warm night.

(M.C.)

Effortless and difficult

Effortless
the flight of the pontos
across Bahia Lake.
Difficult
the flight of humans.
Mechanics on the ground.
Air traffic controllers in the tower.
Pilots on board.
In radio
contact with the earth.
Effortless
the flight of the pontos
across Bahia Lake.
Difficult
the flight of humans.
But higher
further.

(M.C.)

Isla Mujeres II

Whoever wants to can ride on giant turtles
or row out on the sea with fishermen and
watch the swarms of fish.
Whoever wants to can lie down under a coconut palm
and watch iguanas climbing over boards
and bobbing their great lizard heads
up and down
as if they wanted to speak with us.
Whoever wants to can catch crabs in the water
or watch the fish
who rock with the waves
where they collect around the wooden posts
rammed into the water.
Whoever wants to can watch the flight of the pontos birds,
Who scout the coast for fish.
Whoever wants to can look out to the waves, how softly
they beat the shore.
Whoever wants to can let the corn-coloured sand trickle
through his fingers and forget everything for hours.
Whoever wants to can watch the white cloud mountains
in their stately, weightless drift through the warm ether
toward new camping grounds.
Whoever wants to can play chess with the sun
and paint his skin
the colour of coffee beans.
Whoever wants to can lie in a hammock
and undertake a ride through the air á la Munchhausen.
Whoever wants to can swallow the ocean
and submerge in dreams of the universe.
Whoever can, wants to. But who can?

(M.C.)

The pupils

for José Clemente Orozco

When
Orozco died,
they separated
his body
from the easel,
from the glasses
with the pigments,
from tubes and brushes,
from the tape measure
and the knife.

When
Orozco died,
they didn't present him
— like an Indian who's died —
with a little basket
of tortillas
a cup
with agua and
a plate
con pollo
one last time.

When
Orozco died,
they put
his eyeglasses
in a glass case.
And, still staggered,
we look at
the thick glass.

(M.C.)

Rivera

for Diego Rivera

The faded jacket
hangs
one time blue
one time full of work
one time the broad torso
the thick arms of Diego Rivera
taut
over the back
of the chair.

In a brown pot
made of clay
stand the brushes,
beside it, ceremoniously,
a bush of feathers,
duck gray,
as if the whole dance
were yet to come,
as if everything would
continue tomorrow,
as if the colours would
never decline,
as if the standstill
of such a past would
last only this one night.

(M.C.)

Frida Kahlo

Over the bed hangs a mirror.
On the wall,
the images of
Marx, Engels, Lenin, Stalin, and Mao.
In the corner
on the bedpost,
life-size,
homemade,
skeletons and skulls.
Wood.
Garishly painted.

                                        (M.C.)

José Guadalupe Posada

for José Guadalupe Posada

There isn't much
about his life.
Maybe a photo,
discovered
decades later.
There he stood
in front of his studio
'Taller de Grabado'
in Calle de
Santa Ines Nr. 3 in Mexico D.F.
His left hand
in his pants pocket,
the right hand free, almost brushing
against the store window behind him.
Between them
over the round belly
the watch chain.
It appears
as if he walks into the street,
as if he had plenty
or no time at all.
The life of the Mexican people,
the cascade of events,
the fifteen thousand little prints
haven't left him
in peace.
Him,
the folksy woodcut printer
and zinc etcher,
'Mexico's Daumier',
who his land, in 1913,
buried
in a sixth-class grave
reserved for the poor
and who it forgot
and then rediscovered

as chronicler of a lost time.
Him,
who held up
to the living
their petty fraud and violence,
and Calaveras,
Death's heads,
for their improvement.

Leopoldo Mendez,
a Mexican graphic artist,
saw him decades later,
sitting at a table
and watching,
through a window,
dictator Porfirio Diaz' police
clubbing down the populace.
With anger,

with powerful body,
the glance pulled tight into the distance
of past and future,
the left hand balled to a fist,
in the right hand
a graving tool.
Posada
heroically charged up.
Posada was more natural.
He left his studio
and went out to eat.

(M.C.)

Mexico I

Beams carried
for the Cathedral
and the Government Palace.
Whoever couldn't
escape into the mountains,
was given, livestock,
a brand.
Who didn't obey
was hanged.
Then they cashed in.
The advantage
was mutual:
for Cathedral and Government Palace.

(M.C.)

Mexico II

While I look backwards
I fly forwards
While I fly forwards
I look backwards

In only four weeks everything was demanded from my head
and from my body in a country
occupied by Aztecs with bow and arrow
and by the Spaniards on horseback and with iron
and that found its way to a mixture
to Mexico or that discovered itself as this
A plateau on which the bird's glance falls from the heights
to the coasts on two sides of the country, Atlantic and Pacific
Miguel Covarrubias painted everything green
Maybe he was thinking of the life of the snake
a symbol of this country
the maguey cactus another and at the end, the eagle
who must serve, like the lion, for the longing for strength
Land of the flowers on the 'dia del muerte'
and the dancing 'calaveras'
Overpopulated because the economy can't keep up and the
                                                    people
refuse the velocity of this new life
Do the essential, party, and sleep
Nature and fiestas by day and by night
People with black eyes and black hair
The skin is brown
Pastelas, pan and dulcerias, enchiladas, cebollas, and frijoles
everyday foodstuffs tortillas, tortas y tacos
Eating from a tough ground
on which the waters pour in the rainy season
Evenings sometimes mariachi music or the muffled tones of

Sounds of the guajab fruit, of narranjas and mangos
A kingdom of the sun that tears up the earth
Noplaes with their red fruits and maguey
the cactus for tequila
Female plants that sit on the ground like women
and give birth to the land

33

captured by the great Diego Rivera in the paintings of the
Secretaria de Educacion Publica this sitting power
Nature and nature again and again work and again and
again work
In one courtyard work and in the other the parties
And the corrido of the Revolution
Some houses are of tezontle stone
dark red left behind by the volcano
Pedregal in the south of the capital
Dried lava hardened to slag full of resistance
The colours of the Indian wooden masks pull, in their fright,
on the faces: mythology and spell
A colourful line of history in the stairwell of the Palcio
Gobierno
Steps towards the government steps of desire
steps of the claim for life
The line of the Indios, still in a circle, always laden with the
same burden
Above that, history in a line of struggles
Conquistadores in league with the Church
Independence in 1821 and the Reforma
in the middle of the 19th Century
the Revolution of 1910 and then the decades of talk
about the Institutionalized Revolution
The black day of October 2, 1963
Tiatelolco Plaza de tres culturas
The massacre of union members and their families
and of students
four hundred or eight hundred or fifteen hundred
never solved

and the social struggles of this present
within an uncertain future
At the Zocalo, the Cathedral stands cock-eyed
on a stone pedestal on which two corners of the Cross
and four skulls in the four directions of the compass
are still the centre of calm
This capital these fourteen million inhabitants

34

Millions poor, wandering in confusion on the hills of the city
and in the broad plain work and bread, perhaps
In the labyrinths of the city, sheet metal huts
The laundry on the stalks of the maguey
Dogs with bent backs
Millions without anyplace, in the restlessness of an uncertain
                                                    existence
And lots of children, an average of five per family
in the capital and smog
The sacrificial victims of the Aztecs and Mayas
have made way for smoke victims of industry and traffic
Sweetish smell of death in the seven lanes of the
Avenida Revolution and the other arteries of this city
Day and night the whirl of gasses left by the machines
straining urgently toward modern times
Development and underdevelopment desarollo and
                                            subdesarrollo
are the most usual words and the rule of the middle class
Orientation toward the United States and toward Europe,
                                        Standard of Living
plainly written in the books, supposed to be the truth of the
                                                    present
and the truth of these streets
The dogs in the barrios povres run aimlessly about
The dogs of the rich open their throats
and show everyone the teeth of rage
as if he were to blame for their life trimmed of instinct
Walls of the villas walls high and unreachable arriba arriba
Glass shards on the walls
to injure hands
Mexico far away far away from the Paseo Reforma
France was imitated Haußmann's
parade street Champs Élysées
the Palacio Bellas Artes the Mexican Operá
the street Los Insurgentes the street of the insurgents
Far away from Mexico from Popocatepetl and Iztacchuatl
Mountain giants in snow
Far away from the airplane nine thousand metres high

35

Far away from the many talks
all ended

Now, 1985,
disturbed by the pictures of
the earthquake of September 10th
the 4,500 dead
in the middle of the capital
the flickering pictures of
greed and corruption
What appeared treasured
broke in the Colonia Roma
and at the Tlaltelolco Plaza

(M.C.)

3
Books

Plant fibres or animal skin[15]

Since 3300 before our age
the shrub
Since 2000 before
a medical prescription
on papyrus is known
Since 1400 before
parchment

History on
plant fibres and animal skin
here in fragments
once again
on the canvas
as
trapezoid and cuneiform scripts
lined up
reeling 19th
reeling 20th century

(M.C.)

Books I

Books
used to be given not only
hinges
but were also, like shoes,
laced up
The quill stood
up against brutality
as representative of
civilization
blue
or blood-smeared

(M.C.)

Books II

Handwritten
or
printed
line for line
or furiously on
eight-part printers' sheets
In the net of co-ordinates
the text turns
into a window
and the view expands
to time

(M.C.)

Printed area

Forest and
white clouds
The book with the signature
AL 324
has landed in snow
A fountain pen
flies through the air
and turns into a yardstick for
now wild-running time
and to a standstill for the
canvas
taking refuge in the All

(M.C.)

Letter timbering

A book
doesn't rust
and isn't made only
of wood
even if it creaks
in its letter timbering

(M.C.)

Reading

Reading
always has something to do
with bird-flight
thus again and again
this blue-white
feather remnant

(M.C.)

Of reading

He read
between all the signs
Some found this
of use against the dictatorship
One couldn't do more
behind wire fencing
and barred face

(M.C.)

Books have their fates, especially today

Everything used to
take its pitch
from Latin
today from English, Russian, and
Chinese
German, also, once fought abstrusely
using book burning
and the bazooka
for honours
'Habent sua fata libelli'
Wolfgang Nieblich takes up
Italian publishers' sayings
and runs through brown with
blue, ochre, and white
'Habent sua fata libelli'
pro rapido morti

(M.C.)

Visual disturbance

Toward a homage à the transistor
all eyeglasses were
laid down before him
Has the eye abdicated
before the ear?
Have Virginia Woolf
Stefan Zweig Luise Rinser
Kafka and Sartre finally
sunk to the level
of decorative moulding
Less is read now
than 30 years ago you say
I see
I live willy-nilly
but in respect to this change
I still have no answer

                              (M.C.)

Berliner Bookshelves
Pickled Eggs

Delivered up or torn away
from the ageing of the market?
I just don't know
In canning jars
books appear
quite familiarly
as preserves
Consumable only for
another two or three years

(M.C.)

Nothing is in its place any more

The surgeon, too,
no longer rescues
the book
As a rule
he cuts
vital parts out
from the living body
and is less and less
in his place

(M.C.)

Lead poisoning

Wolfgang Nieblich
found a white skull
openable on hinges at the top
and also the cause of death
mass of lead

(M.C.)

The complete works

Height 43
Width 20
It did amount to something
in life
tied up by the publisher
The package now
stands there
powdered and
blackened
with a wooden grip
from Mother
for some descendant
to journey
Handy-pack

(M.C.)

4
Step Human
into this
World

Step human into this world

Script from abstraction
brought back into space
and extended to sculpture
Tripod of Pythia
proverbs over the Mediterranean
mumbled toward Asia
Heavy breathing
over the gaping split in the earth
caught in the bars of the
centuries
I-Ging
and from all three sides the sign
'the human'
again and again bent apart
through bones and
instinctual charge

Everything has remained
open until today
despite cross
despite yellow sun
despite Crescent Moon
despite the Goddess Reason
despite the October Revolution
Too many pagodas and
towers athwart
Far East and Near West
swords and archways
and everywhere long-distance trains right through
the
I-continents
I-Europe
I-Asia
I-America
I-Africa
No you interplanetary space

The human is responsible for
his
for the time after the umbilical cord
for his voice
four- or two- or three-legs
in the riddle of the sphinx
steep flight
but what protects him
from plunging

Circle and square
are merely two abstractions
in the confusion of signs
The gravity of a gong
can no longer keep up
with the squeaking of electronics
Longing was applied
and shot to pieces in wars

Without stable fastenings
nothing stands
The time of flowers standing alone
is gone
What secures
impedes
What restricts the stride
gives the legs
their strength in the first place
But somewhere the promise is waiting
the future is waiting
some warming power is waiting

(M.C.)

Beast-end

Wind in Knossos
8 anemos
Wind in Hvar and Dubrovnic
vjetar
Winds in the East and West
Aeras
The Minotaur is everywhere
Leap from the beast
into the human
Leaps from the Archaic
to the 'big mouth mask',
from the muffled
to the loud and into the
Egyptian and Phoenician,
Greek and Roman,
Arabic and Slavic,
from the roar
into meditation
Forward Backward Afterward

Red long tongue
Leap to the ideol
Which mask did Clytemnestra wear?
Leap of a bull
into Heaven
A startled bull-child
rams into a chair leg
Apis bulls
From the hatch of the little
gable window
white-red glimpse
the bull has stepped
from the shrine
the ibis
the locust
the scarab

Forehead-nose
Gamboling
Woman-slits
Green Medusa face
Terror sits in the body
and doesn't leave

All lovey-doveyness
pressed down
to Adam and Eve as beginning
away from Fotofix
away from two moments
garnered from hours
away from the beast
away from theology

The 'energy fetish' is made of
steel
At Thyseen, waste in the container
Aside from Herakles' overbold Argonauts
rigidified
to iron and the end of their story
The Hero is not fixated on the
taboo
Courage of the Hero
Herakles wanders about the Mediterranean
and defeats the bull
outside and inside himself
Doubled struggle
doubled civilization
Adam becomes a consumer and the bull
beef

Homeric laughter
that a mask hangs in the washroom
or poker-faced men
The 'Nubian Princess'
is sewn shut at mouth and nose

Ponal and bird sand are changed
to skin
Meditation in white and black
and blue and violet

Something specific and overpowering
no longer exists
It doesn't lie down for the night
in a grimace anymore
Evil now has,
despite all continuing ignominy,
the status of a chimera

Herakles fixates the eye of the Pythia
to defeat her
I Ging
The Book of Changes simultaneously
openings beastlike and
funnel-shaped
Apollo still streaks
Demeter still metamorphizes
Daphne still runs
Everything ends like it does in some paintings
done by Diego Rivera in the forties
at the knot of a branch

Scrap heap on the Panke River
the two horns have sprung away
from the bull's head
The vigor of the act is lessened
The Argonauts have now
developed into space by a turning
Tanks are outmoded
Weaponry is outmoded
Apollo is defeated not by the funnel
but by the charm of Europa

A blood-red Dionysos no longer fits in
with the times
The cult of the Apis bull was crossed out
just like the stereotype of the paddlewheel
of a Mississippi riverboat
ten years old and
the sight of the concentration camps' mass graves
could not be contained by George Brassen's chansons
Murderously, the dignity of man
was slaughtered
Relapse into the realm of beasts
Beast-end when?

(M.C.)

Stones

First close-by
pebbles
as the simplest memory
something of me

then the distant
the strange
past the waystones
to Carrara and
off to the
Mediterranean
to bone stones

In the currents
of the veining
pain will be
polished to light
the grainy
to skin

For the duration
a part of the body
suffices
and the refusal of
fingers

Flesh and bones
have been
submerged
in the sight of
medicine and art

part of the solution
may be from the Old Testament
or Islamic

(M.C.)

Kurt Schwitters

What others made in colours
he translated in shavings of paper
newspapers and
tickets

Consonance in
wood
shreds of clothes
past and
tapestries

Instead of grounding the canvas
he cut out
instead of painting
he dipped into colour
instead of brushing to and fro
he glued together

(M.C.)

Merz

Merz
had nothing to do
with the god of war
but meant
'to create relations
preferably between
all things of the world'
said Kurt Schwitters
and this also was
Dada

(M.C.)

Block letters and garden

Everything is white in the beginning
When the block letters leave
the thoughts behind mechanically
as lines to the left
black or red
I step in to the right
with leaves of lavender and paper
or with blue colours and
coloured hatching
or I go tracking with
green and red and yellow body hatching
Flower petals from the garden
I glue on, too, and
remnants of lacquered paper and tin foil
in all colours
and scraps of thrown-out tulle
and silk

When I see
how blue turns pale
and green turns brown
and even textile remnants unravel
I'm not disconsolate about time
but start a new picture
there everything is still
white

(M.C.)

5
Egypt

I am the God-spine inside the tamarisk

proverb 42, line 8
Egyptian Book of the Dead

Nagi Naguib

When he picked us up from the airport
it was three o'clock in the morning
When, in the morning in a suburb of Cairo,
we woke
he had already initiated us
into Fool
the Egyptian bean dish with oil and lemon
When he left us the key to the apartment
the Egyptian sun had already foamed
and, with lame and yet ever more stabbing steps,
reached its zenith

He explained from his balcony
what Egypt is
and looked out over a square
dirt and lawn plaza
standing wild in front of the building
'It will never be finished', he said and smiled
as if he were secretly glad
as if he himself
and, by extension, Egypt
were this awkward thing
The sprinklers are always there
but one corner is under water
the others are dry and hard
and in the middle grass grows but scantily
All the trees planted years ago
look bent and slight
and will hardly mature

But thus he loved the country from which he came
and criticized it too
he
who had lived the last twenty years in Berlin
and studied European culture and Fascist barbarism
and who, a specialist,
translated Egyptian literature
into the German language

but not German into the Egyptian
he
who is married to a German woman:
Christa
and who has a son:
Jonas
he
who has long since attained the qualifications
of a Professor
without a job
as a pioneer of Egyptian culture in Germany
When we, in the crowd in Cairo,
stood awhile on El Tahrir Square
and looked into the chaos of traffic
slowly bumping toward order
a quick shudder ran through him
'I feel as if in a foreign country here'
the words broke out of him
He rushed with us to the magazine 'Al Mussawar'
for which he regularly wrote articles
and delivered a new manuscript

                                        (M.C.)

Man

Born
from the Nile mud
brown and dirty
millennia old
it's that simple

(M.C.)

Wish or exhaustion

We walk with heavy shoes
through the rooms of the
Egyptian Museum
and finally
set ourselves down,
statues

(M.C.)

Egyptian script

Boats on the Nile
the rudder at an angle
reaching downward
Snakes flat
with their long body
brought into a line
plum-shaped head
many spots
and always the feeling of
reptiles
Current and water

(M.C.)

Sarcophagus

The coffin
fitted to
the form of the body
Remnants of flesh and bones
seem to push
the hull outward
I stand there half
like a bird
without wings
featherless
for the other half
I am a back
What elsewhere lies flat
is stood up here
land stands
like a grandfather clock
black ciphers on white
1302 or 6289
timeless
without a plumbline
leaned against the wall

(M.C.)

Pyramids at Giza

Out of the dusky
desert light
three hats emerge
on which the sun's rays
slide along
dragging like camels
In place of the smoothly polished
light on the stone facing
of Tura chalk
the far-wandered sand
settles in for a long stay
in Numilite stone
or comes
for a short visit

(M.C.)

Cheops payramid

Bent like the
Pharaoh's slaves
we climb with bowed backs
— as if the burden
of the stony work
were still upon us —
the wooden walkways
to the open sarcophagus
up into the pyramid
and pull ourselves hand over hand,
after a short
listless look over the
naked walls of the
empty burial chamber
that stinks of sweat and shit,
back down into free space

(M.C.)

Pyramids

The pyramids already stood in the desert
before the first were ever
built
by the slaves of the Pharaohs
and they still stand
Nature has left them
as a blueprint
for their original
millennia-old grave

(M.C.)

Idu's grave

In the Mastaba of Idu
our words begin
rumbling like
jet engines
but the echo
comes from the sixth dynasty
out of the cavern of time

(M.C.)

Oh yes — a European tourist with closed eyes

He stood calmly at the wall
with arms crossed
in the burial chamber
of the Chephren Pyramid
and sank
thousands of years back
into the fourth dynasty
while
no one else
could stand it there
in the thick
turgid air
and the latrine smell
of people and animals

(M.C.)

Emptiness

On the edge of the desert
I pitch
my pyramid
like the Pharaohs
and
a few dozen metres
under the earth
below the gable roof
of a burial chamber
I drink tea
Then I climb up
the steps again
bent as always
and fold this pyramid
back up again

(M.C.)

Sphinx

She came
in the night
she departed again
in the night
when did I see her
with her smashed nose
and smashed mouth
I don't know
when she lost her face
I will never learn
what she is
I will never know
neither with rising
nor with setting sun

Late in the morning
when a shadow
lays itself down on the right side of her cheek
and wanders along
the broad Egyptian chin below
then I no longer know
can she stand up to the sun
lying on the frontier
between desert and
Nile mud

(M.C.)

Deficiencies

That Egypt
is only as wide
as the Nile
contradicted my
starting point
That the Nile
so flagrantly
means life
and the desert beside it
death
I didn't even imagine
as a possibility
That present-day Egypt
is a poor country
I didn't used to believe
nor did the newspapers
mention it

(M.C.)

Egypt

Everything is made of clay
It is well-known
that the Nile sludge
sun-dried to tiles
is used in building houses
That Man
is formed of clay
stands in Genesis
in the Hebrew Testament

This myth started and spread
from here
and from the Sinai Desert
from Mesopotamia and Persia

(M.C.)

No reversal of the universe — Sunset in Aswan

When the ball of the sun
lies
exactly on the horizon line
it doesn't take two minutes
for it to go down
For a few seconds we imagine
that it immediately
takes the opposite direction and
returns
This wish is inspired
by the 'Stella Beer'
we're drinking
in the garden of the Old Cataract Hotel
But just as quickly
as this fantasy arose
we shift
and wait as always for the morning
and this idea
reversing the course of the universe
sinks from view

(M.C.)

Ramses in Abu Simbel

To sit like this
and look over the Nile
elephantiasis in one's legs
a jar on one's head
with the humming of the
wars
and a paw of a hand
on one's thigh

(M.C.)

Illusions of a European

After a week
brown as an Egyptian
after two weeks
dark as a Nubian
after three weeks
black as Africa

(M.C.)

I prefer Winnetou[16]

With his left hand Ramses holds
a stone wedge
on the head of a prisoner
With his right
he pounds without mercy
to split it
In another fresco relief
he slays ten at once
I prefer Winnetou

(M.C.)

Fear of being overlooked
Abu Simbel and Osiris

Four thousand years ago
I placed myself
fat and awkward
in the hall
six times twelve metres high
so that you
observer from the 20th century
cannot
overlook me

(M.C.)

Cynical

No one speaks of
the slaves
who built
the temples of
Philae
Luxor or
Karnak
Why should they
slavery
has been abolished, hasn't it

(M.C.)

It knows why —
In the bus through the Nubian Desert

The fly
comes again
and again
to my arms and legs
and to my head
It doesn't fly
out into the desert
It knows why

(M.C.)

The Botanical Island in the Nile in Aswan or the slyness of the colonial master

Monuments of stone or iron
are, when the time comes,
torn down from the pedestal
Lord Kitchener realized this
so he left
an island with plants
instead

(M.C.)

Luxor I

Your name is glorified
Not only the horses
Of your carriages limp
The people
Also go lame
Like everywhere in Egypt
Your bakshish glance
Takes its toll

(M.C.)

Luxor II

Every day you stir up
unspeakable dust
and derange
the people's lungs
with dried Nile mud
Dirt-hole, some will curse you
and he who believes
that black lung comes only from
mining
learns something new
The colossal columns of the temples of
Karnak
are completely useless to you
the colourful images of the afterlife
in the Kings' graves in East Thebes
and the free-standing colossus of Memnon
But I'm already retreating
if I say
stone and dust hold each other in balance
Your name in any case
promises more
And when I think about it
this constant bakshish glance
here too takes
its toll on me

(M.C.)

The el-Medina
City of the necropolis workers

The tourists
arrive as a mule caravan
and are greeted
with the barks of the remaining
wild dogs of the
necropolis workers
The curs briefly interrupt
sleep
to turn yapping
toward the shadow places
of their masters
dead for 3,500 years

(M.C.)

Memnon's Colossus
The two sitting statues of Amenophis III

To look the rising sun
in the eyes
means
to turn one's back on the setting
To look eastward
means
to expect everything from the dawn
and nothing or nothing more
from the dusk
When they sit so erectly
they are actually at their zenith
and it makes no difference
if it's day or night
morning or evening
when the sun heads toward farewell
and young Egyptian women
in lemon yellow clothes and
stuffed-up noses
offer dolls for 50 piasters

What here was cut with blows
to colossi
each from its own single sandstone block
21 metres high
was regarded as a Wonder of the World
even if Teje the wife
and Mutemuja the mother
standing
reach only to the knee
of the seated Amenophis
The feet are scrawled upon
with the Greek and Latin sentences
of ancient tourists

(M.C.)

Menon's Colossus in East Thebes
One of the Seven Wonders of the World

Many were here
Millions of pairs of eyes have rested
on the two smashed faces
of one and the same Amenophis III
and on the hip
damaged 2000 years ago
in an earthquake
For a few seconds
the glance of curiosity wafted across them
before travelling further

(M.C.)

Islamic cemetery in the country

Lots of little mounds of sand
and at the head end
a bent, pointed
stone
as if stuck there by chance

(M.C.)

Islamic death?

With death
what lives
lost
at one blow
even its name

(M.C.)

Islamic cemetery in Cairo

Those who can afford it
finance life
even after death
with land and a house
in which they can
occasionally spend
the night with a lover

(M.C.)

Pharoahs

The divine symbols
are balanced
on top of the head
That is, after all
a burden

(M.C.)

Lawgiver

Thutmosis III
in the Kings' Tombs at Luxor
with the papyrus

the Moses of Michelangelo
in St. Peter's
with a folio
that Christians presume
to call the Old
instead of the Hebrew Testament

(M.C.)

The Pope is the last Pharaoh

The Pope's tiara
this overgrown bonnet
is taken from Osiris and Amenophis
from Egypt
The only difference is
the Egyptian one slopes backward
while the Pope's sits
erect as a board

But the encyclopedia corrects me
Tiara
'originally a high, tapering
covering for the head with a gold ring (Kidarsis)
worn by Persian kings; Papal Crown
since 1300 with three rings (Shepherd's, Teacher's,
and Priest's Offices)'
But the cultures of the ancient Egyptians
could hardly be distinguished
from those of the Persians

(M.C.)

Birth defect

That Christendom
was unable
to hold its own
in the places of its origin
and also
in the neighbouring regions
gives it no peace
to this day
and is felt
in Rome
to be a defect and burden

(M.C.)

The beetle of Luxor

Now he is gone
only his picture remains
material in memory
intangible
like there at the newsstand
on the dusty main street
this beetle from Luxor
hand sewn on the cloth
on a black background
in an ornamental frame
scarab of the God of
the rising sun
for forty pounds

(M.C.)

Coast road on the Red Sea

There's nothing
even if, for a while
a pipeline accompanies
and electric power masts
mark the route
or red-black cannisters of tar
stand around
used up and of no use
or isolated tufts
on the remaining
little hills of sand on a sand-spout
there are only
sand and stones
from Morghada to Suez

(M.C.)

Yahya Hakki

The first thing he says is
that in the '20s in Egypt
the cigarettes were flat
and not until the Europeans and Americans came
were there round ones
that in the past instead of packs
individual cigarettes were sold
so that anyone
even he with only a few piasters
could have a smoke
which today would be disadvantageous
since the Egyptian government
like many other governments in the world
is conducting a campaign
against smoking
and that in the past strings
were pulled on needles through
the veins of the tobacco leaves
to stretch them
while
they dried

He looks like Jean-Paul Sartre
the French writer
without the eyes akimbo
but he is even smaller in stature
When he sits in the armchair
his left leg slides under the right
like a clown's
or as if he were repeating
with his 81 years
the old Muslim-style sitting
In his room
hangs a portrait
in shades of yellow and gray
the outlines of the head
are white
Under it

as if on a blackboard
two meanings are explained
with two colours rectangles
Yellow stands for
strong intellect
grey
for devotion
mixed with affection
he says

Classical Arabia
knows no theatre and no literature in prose
but overflows
with the power of poetry
Once there were, he starts to recount
four unmarried women
their parents were already
getting desperate
and so when everything else had been tried
in vain
they got a poet
and shortly after
each of them found
a husband
and each of them a new roof

He is afraid
of the rapid growth
of the Egyptian population
a lion
that runs and runs
and whom one must constantly
and quickly throw
something to eat
so that it doesn't reach
and devour Egypt
What he admires is
resistance

the self-confidence of the Copts
who, during the conquest
of Egypt by the Arabs
refused
to convert to Islam
and the self-confidence of the
Jews
who for centuries
scattered in all countries
tenaciously awaited
their unification
and the return
to Jerusalem
but they shouldn't
take the land away
from the Palestinians

Socialism, in his opinion
is suspect
it sees in people
only a life
and no longer a living being

So, snow-white by now
Yahya Hakki smokes
an Egyptian cigarette
he
who created
the tale
'The Oil Lamp of Umm Maschim'
and
'The Postmaster'
he
the former lawyer
and archivist
diplomat
and first director of the
Department of Fine Arts

founded in 195
he the writer
for a new Egypt
Yahya Hakki
in Sharia El Ghazali
in Heliopolis

(M.C.)

Ah, Cairo

Ah, Cairo
are you ruined in the air
and not beginning
to go under the earth until 1986
by building the subway
like Mexico D.F. at the end of the '60s
you will hardly unburden yourself

Your car drivers are acrobats
but it's not enough
simply to get through the tangle
and home
alive
you will suffocate soon
on the plague
you leave behind daily
through your exhaust pipes

Ah, Cairo
where has your art of
green places and parks
beautiful squares and fountains
gone
Do you want to forbid
palms and oleanders to step on the grass
and if you don't go that far
do you want
to finish them off
with ever more new buildings and freeways

Ah, Cairo
who can much longer
stand remaining in you
when you burst
all your seams
and the people
move into your cemeteries
finding a place for themselves

next to the dead
themselves half dead
or in sheet metal huts
between garbage dumps and mountains of rubble
and dwell
in the kilns of dead pottery shops

Ah, Cairo
you build and build
and at the same time leave everything as it is
There are always millions of people
underway but why and for what
it simply isn't the case
that more happens on the street
than in European metropoles
merely because of the hot weather
Something isn't right
in the present run of your history
But that you don't go wrong
I mean not the goats
that wander through your suburbs
or the beep-beep and wonk-wonk
of your horns
even if it is starting
to get on my nerves

Ah, Cairo
in the late afternoon there was nothing
to be seen of the sunset
everything is that unclear in your plague of smog
even if I admit to you
that, in the big cities of Europe, I seldom give
these everyday natural wonders
a glance
Believe me
I was hopelessly stuck
not only at the Central Train Station
near the Ramses statue

Ah, Cairo
I'm not hoarse
when I speak
or even squawk like this
frightening for others
although your murk of soot and dust
tortures my throat daily
and my bones are getting old
It isn't just the Americans
who make you sigh
and the Soviets
whose promise to help
certainly wasn't entirely unselfish
you have firmly
if politely
sent home
If I see it right
it is you yourself
who can dissolve the slums
and the rubble and the dust
and the noise

Ah, Cairo
if your ears weren't
already stopped up
you would go early tomorrow morning
and get to work
I believe
you would manage it

(M.C.)

Even in death

A camel
has died in the desert
Even in Death
as a mere skeleton it kneels
to be mounted

(M.C.)

6
Malta:
The One
& The Other

Malta I

Television antennas stand,
long-stemmed artificial flowers,
up above the roofs
as if the place
were surrounded by mountains
Fishermen throw the fish
bread in the ocean beforehand
Buses are painted green
and white
Boats bob up and down

(M.C.)

Malta II

Despite the crusts of bread,
the fisherman hasn't
outwitted any fish yet
Pigeons practise a
communal slalom
through the antenna forest
The flag is red and white
A fish bites
The fish body wriggles

(M.C.)

Malta III

The referee's whistle
intervenes in the game
just before noon
Churches prop themselves up
between the buildings
A motorcycle whines
on the pier
celebrating Sunday

(M.C.)

Oh sea

Oh sea
to listen to you
gnawing away at stone
Precisely because I
already hear your roar
I can follow you
no more

(M.C.)

Limestone

The chalk
in Malta is
yellow
A choice
between
mocca cream
and
vanilla pudding

(M.C.)

In Malta

In Malta,
clouds conceal
the moon
time after time
It returns
as a host wafer
and as a wheel
of the celestial wagon
of the prophet
Elijah

(M.C.)

Malta IV

In the ether wave war
between
Occident
and
Orient
Malta
has
remained
a Christian
bulwark

(M.C.)

Malta V

For every village
a Cathedral
On the bus' rear
licence plate holder
a stylized lily
that penetrates
a horseshoe
If that isn't lucky

(M.C.)

20th century

for Latin students

Verbum Dei
Motor
factum est

(M.C.)

Endless time

The Phoenicians
cut down
the forests of the island
Endless time
But the inhabitants of
Malta
carry the burden to this day

(M.C.)

Refuge Castle in Rabat

The night grows because
down in the valley
the chain of lights
are ignited
and in Sliema
fireworks begin

(M.C.)

Hagar Quim I
(Hadjar Eem)

Erected
stones
Indignation
of the human
toward the
apes
First
distance

(M.C.)

Lino Spiteri
— former Minister of Finances
of the Labour Party

In front of the old portraits
in the House of Parliament
he stands himself
like a statesman
He is greeted everywhere
He earns
the respect of the Maltese
a beloved man

(M.C.)

Rottman's Bar

The old Maltese
takes his dentures
in his left hand
and sings
Italian arias
and English operas
It's hardly surprising
Sicily is only
90 kilometres away
and the English
colonial rule
until 1814
is only a few years
distant

(M.C.)

Malta VI

The English
have left their old colonies
behind
as trading outposts
One drives on the left side
Every second tavern
is a pub
and one deposits the
postcards
in red English
mailboxes

(M.C.)

Calypso

Who knows
whether Odysseus
arrived
at the island of Gozo
and, entangled by Calypso,
didn't come loose
for three years
If he didn't manage
after three years
then it was seven
Those are the rhythms
in which separations between
men and women occur

(M.C.)

Mnajdra

In the late afternoon,
six women
from the alternative scene
with blue backpacks
arrive on the south coast of
Malta
They camp nights
in the ruins of the
Mnajdra Temple from the
Megalith Culture
Two in the loins
two in the breasts
and two in the head
of the finally found
great old
pregnant Mother

(M.C.)

Malta VII

A chicken
constantly plucked by conquerors
First the Phoenicians
dined on it
At last the English
let them go
treeless
brick for brick
The few birds and
rabbits
are shot down

(M.C.)

7
China

War on Tianamen Square

against Teng Hsiao Ping

Just as you rise
you set.

Just born
the light already out.

The idea
of an old man
still capable to run a country
you destroyed.

Why did you not resign
and stop after so many years of breathing?
After so many years of endeavour
why did you not retire
like millions of elderly people before?

Why did you not sit on a garden bench
or on a balcony
competing with the sun early in the
morning
or with the birds
on your last flight?
Now you have stained with blood
the end of your life
in the midst of China's hope
in the midst of the city's heart
in the midst of Tianamen Square.

Now you have declared war
not on your obstinacy
but on young lives and on students.

Now — without consolation for the
relatives of thousands of victims —

122

you have spoiled China's image for decades
and in the eyes of many for good.

Go and resign today.

In the face of the dead on Tianamen Square
and in the capital
your vision of a future life
is hopelessly outdated

and you have fallen out irreconcilably
with yourself and with mankind.

(I.S.)

Dear Albert

Dear Albert,

Nothing quicker than history swallowing us,
nothing faster than events overtaking,
nothing worse than our ignorance
and yet — some things in this life are only bearable because
of it.

This Tianamen Square on which we walked like children
looking here and there,
the thousands of photos on which we posed rather naively
the plates which we used to take photos of others posing.

This Mao Tse Tung — whose victims of the 'Cultural Revolution'
we met everywhere — of whom we did not know
whether he still was normal or whether he had developed
magalomania over the last 10 years.

What was there in the catafalque? And we walked around it and
around the master of the mummies. And we remembered Moscow or
thought about the worship of relics by the catholic church,
her heroes and 'saints'. How close felt Bavaria despite the
distance?

Socialism or whatever life is called there, presented itself
with an uncertainty and — seen from this angle or from the
cathedral of the 'genuine' religions — as an ersatz religion.
Apparently capitalism handled religion far better than
socialism, despite its alleged existence in reality.

This distant look in the eyes. This deafening noise in the
ears. This dust beneath the feet. These torrents. These
erosions reaching the sea. These self-delusions. These colours
first time on the market. The blue and green jackets. The
single trees. This wind.

We did not waste one thought on 'from this generation' when
in discussions at the University of Shanghai or with students

in Beijing, or when I read Berlin-poems for those who wanted to open for their lives new doors far wider than their parents before them.

And how is Cong Weixi who wrote about his suffering in the country during the Cultural Revolution, about his detention? And what does the passionate Zhang Ji do who was amazed at the Christian taboo regarding abortion considering the rapidly increasing world population of presently 5 billion people?

Tianamen Square. It is as if you pass a house which collapses behind you. What are these spasms that Stalinism is still causing in Asia? What worth is a human life in Asia? Have we been demoralized in Europe by Fascism and Asia by Japan? But after 50 years.

A journey has come to an end. To an end have come the illusions. How could we as part of the people of this world community still enter Tianamen Square without loosing our honour or tread on it? A journey has come to an end. To an end have come the illusions.

Regards,

Olav

(I.S.)

Notes:

1. The House Nr. 4a in Berlin Tiergarten Sigismundstrasse is the last old one there. It was to have been demolished to make way for an ensemble of new museums called 'Kulturforum'. The poem was a contribution to saving it. After a seven-year struggle by a number of citizens the house is now integrated in the plans for this region, situated near the Potsdamer Platz.

2. Berlin celebrated its 750-year jubilee in 1987, but East and West Berlin celebrated separately.

3. Potsdamer Platz: perhaps the busiest square in Europe prior to World War II. Now a dead field cut by the Berlin Wall.

4. Weimar Republic: name of the German state between 1919 and 1933 between the fall of the Kaiser and the rise of Hitler.

5. So-called 'Drittes Reich': the time of Hitler (1933–1945).

6. 'Germania': Hitler and Speer (Hitler's chief architect) planned to built a new monumental Berlin around a seven-kilometre road stretching north to south ('Nord-Süd-Achse'). Thousands of houses would be destroyed to make way for a hall bigger than the dome of St. Peter's in Rome with the capacity to hold 100,000 people, a hall in honour of soldiers ('Soldatenhall') and new gigantic buildings to house the ministries. When complete (by the end of a 'successful' war around 1950) Berlin would be re-named 'Germania'. It would be the capital of Europe, with all other European states reduced to slave states.

7. 'Wannsee Conference': Here it was decided to exterminate the Jewish population of Europe.

8. Prinz Albrechstrasse: the most feared street in Berlin during the Nazi era, because here people were tortured.

9. S-Bahnhof: the station of the 'Berliner Stadtbahn'.

10. Stadt-Mitte and Prenzlauer Berg: districts in East Berlin.

11. J. Stirling: postmodern English architect.

12. 'Being of what is' ('Sein des Seienden'): abstract formula of the German philosopher Martin Heidegger. He was nominated 'Rektor' in a German university and gave philosophical backing to the Nazi system.

13. 'Trabant': East German popular car; literally 'satellite' or 'follower'.

14. 'Critical Theory': a variant of Western Marxism fashionable in the 1960s.

15. The poems were suggested by pictures and objects by the painter and object-artist Wolfgang Nieblich, West Berlin, and by the catalogue 'The book as object', which shows works from 1984. The titles of some of the poems are taken from those of the artist's works.

16. Winnetou is a figure in Karl Mays's popular adventure stories, classical literature for young people in German-speaking countries. An Indian, he is the partner of Old Shatterhand, a white frontiersman. Together they are heroes standing for the good Indian and the good white respectively.

Other Titles from Germany Published by Forest Books

AN ANTHOLOGY OF SORBIAN POETRY

Translated & Edited by Robert Elsie

UNESCO Collection of Representative Works

The very existence of the Sorbs, a Slavic minority in Germany, may be a surprise to many. The literature of this tiny national minority in East Germany, presented in English translation for the first time by Robert Elsie, has made its own modest contribution to the mosaic of European culture, a tiny and quite unique voice in a great choir.'

ISBN 0 948259 72 8   paper £6.95   96 pages

THE PIED POETS

Contemporary Verse of the Transylvanian and Danube Germans of Romania

Selected & Translated by Robert Elsie

The Pied Poets marks the passing of the 'fifth German literature', that of the German minority of Romania.

This bilingual anthology of contemporary verse, introduced and translated by Robert Elsie, plunges into the hearts and minds of the Transylvanian Saxons and Danube Swabians, who once set off with pioneer fervour to 'go east, young man' in order to found a better Germany, and are now returning to their origins, some with now a more fervent hope of a better Romania.

ISBN 0 948259 77 9   paper £8.95   208 pages

Olav Münzberg
Wilmersdorfer Str. 106
10 629 Berlin

T. 0049/30/3242341
email: olav.muenzberg@t-online.de